It's Your Health!

Sex
and Relationships

ADAM HIBBERT

W
FRANKLIN WATTS
LONDON•SYDNEY

First published in 2004 by Franklin Watts
96 Leonard Street, London EC2A 4XD

Franklin Watts Australia
45-51 Huntley Street, Alexandria, NSW 2015

Series editor: Sarah Peutrill
Designed by: Pewter Design Associates
Series design: Peter Scoulding
Illustration: Roger Gorringe
Picture researcher: Sophie Hartley
Series consultant: Wendy Anthony, Health Education Unit, Education Service, Birmingham City Council
Picture credits: © Paul Baldesare/Photofusion: 4, 19b, 24, 32, 40, 41b, 45. Photos from
www.JohnBirdsall.co.uk: 11t, 14, 15b, 35, 39, 41t. © Mark Campbell/Photofusion: 10. © Paul
Doyle/Photofusion: 29. John Foxx/Alamy: 34. Chris Fairclough: 11b, 12, 15t, 18, 31, 38b. Adam Hart-
Davis/Science Photo Library: 23. image100/Alamy: 19t. Image Source/Alamy: 30. Image State/Alamy: 8b.
Bob Jones Photography/Alamy: 16. © Ute Klaphake/Photofusion: 37. © Brian Mitchell/Photofusion: 9.
Jeroen Oerlemans/Rex Features: 36. Phanie Agency/Rex Features: 27. © Ulike Preuss/Photofusion: 8t, 38t.
Rex Features: 13. SIPA/Rex Features: 17, 22, 28. © Libby Welch/Photofusion: 33.
Every attempt has been made to clear copyright. Should there be any inadvertent omission, please apply to
the publisher for rectification.

The Publisher would like to thank the Brunswick Club for Young People, Fulham, London for their help
with this book. Thanks to our models, including Grace Hurren, Daisy Lillis, Tori Lopez, Paige Morgan,
Elliott Scott, Aimee Wise, Morgan Wheeler, Spencer Thoroughgood, Elliot Vinel, Stevie Waite and Eva Webb.

A CIP catalogue record for this book is available from the British Library.

ISBN 0 7496 5568 2

Printed in Malaysia

This title conforms with guidance from:
The Sex Education Forum (UK)
DfEE Sex and Relationship Education Guidance (0016/2000)

'It's Your Experience' quotes reprinted with permission from SEX, ETC., the US national newsletter and
website (www.sexetc.org) written by teens, for teens, on sexual health issues, published by the Network for
Family Life Education at Rutgers, The State University of New Jersey.

Contents

Sex and relationships

As we change from children to young adults, our bodies and our feelings change. For all our lives so far, our strongest relationships were with our parents and family members. By the age of eight or nine, we begin to make close friends outside the family. These friendships are different from the relationships we have with our family. They are often intense or unpredictable.

Depending on their cultural traditions or religious beliefs, some young people may decide to avoid all sexual contact until marriage.

Sexual maturity

Just as we begin to discover how to be friends with others, our growing bodies make things more complicated. As children, we know we are male or female, and even try acting like a 'man' or a 'woman'. But we can also ignore those roles, and the worries about how well we fit them.

Between the ages of around 11 and 16 years old, our bodies mature. The sexual roles we played at before are suddenly a lot more real.

Sticking out

Most of us know what it's like to be teased about our sex role – boys in particular tease each other for being 'girls' if they do not play their sex role by the 'rules'.

Around puberty we may be more sensitive to such attitudes because we are less confident about these new aspects of ourselves. It can seem easier to conform to pressure from peers than to defend how we feel, especially if our sexuality breaks the 'rules'.

In our teens we develop new friendships. Some of us may feel awkward or at ease with members of the opposite sex.

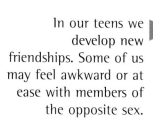

Although schools try to educate us about sex and relationships, we also learn from parents, peers, books and television.

It's your opinion

Why do you think people tend to tease or bully those that are 'different'? Should people try to express their differences or conform to what is normal?

Sex education

Every one of us has to find our own way through these challenges – to learn from our own mistakes. Apart from some faith teachings, there is no absolutely right or wrong way to become a sexually mature young adult. But there are some simple facts, especially about health and pregnancy, which can help us skip some of the nastiest surprises.

It's our health

Learning about sex and relationships is important. Unless we know how to look after ourselves, our health is at risk. Sex may have serious consequences, from pregnancy to fatal diseases. We can take responsibility for our health by finding out more and being ready to protect ourselves. Knowing health facts can help us to be more confident and relaxed. The more we know, the more sure we can be of ourselves and of others.

It's your opinion

It can be frustrating to listen to someone tell us things we already know. But the privacy that surrounds sex in most societies means that many people, especially children, learn quite a bit of what they know from rumour rather than good information. Take a look at the chart (right) and find out how you and your friends compare with the results.

This chart shows how well-informed young people feel about sex – and how comfortable they are discussing sex with their parents.

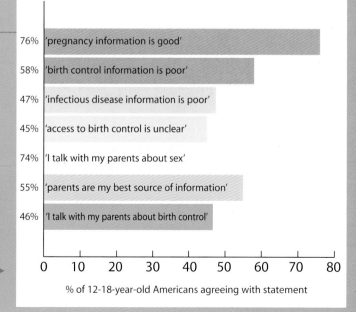

	%
'pregnancy information is good'	76%
'birth control information is poor'	58%
'infectious disease information is poor'	47%
'access to birth control is unclear'	45%
'I talk with my parents about sex'	74%
'parents are my best source of information'	55%
'I talk with my parents about birth control'	46%

% of 12-18-year-old Americans agreeing with statement

Independence

With friends, we can have more freedom than we do with our families. Friends are more likely to see us as equals, whereas parents still tell us what to do. Parents can find it hard to appreciate us as individuals, rather than their little girl or boy. That is why, as we start to seek independence from our families, and become closer to friends, it can be easier to start to explore who we are – and who we would like to be.

Teenage friendships are built around shared tastes and interests, but it is still possible for each of us to develop our own personal style.

Defining ourselves

Around puberty, it is not just our bodies that change. Our personalities change, too. We start to develop new interests and tastes. In the past, we may have agreed with our parents or siblings about all sorts of things, from clothes and music to politics. Now, as we become individuals, we start to have our own tastes, interests and opinions. Often, we find that these are better understood by our friends than by our families.

Friends and partners

When we want to talk through our most personal experiences, we need someone that we can trust. That is why many of us have best friends. By sharing our secrets with them, we develop an intimacy that feels as close as – or even closer than – any family bond.

Another way to achieve intimacy is through a sexual relationship. Some of us feel even closer to a partner than to our best friend, because we are sharing such a private, special experience. Others find friends are more reliable, because relationships with them are more likely to last.

Parental control

As we start to grow away from our parents, they usually recognise that they have to give us more freedom. This can be hard – they may worry about us putting ourselves into dangerous situations. Sometimes, parents' rules can seem over-protective or even selfish.

From our parents' point of view, things look different. They are responsible for us, by law, at least until we are 16 years old, and in some places until we are 21 years old. This means that society requires them to look after us.

It's good if we can confide in our boyfriend or girlfriend, but it may take time to build up enough trust.

It's your opinion

Do your parents set a time that you have to come home by? Can you think of any reasons why they might do this to look after your best interests? Are there any ways that an 'in-by' time makes life easier for them? Do you think you would set the same rules if you were in their shoes?

Relationships with parents can take a nose-dive, but it's not helpful for either side to sulk or fly off the handle.

It's your experience

'With most of my problems, I feel much more comfortable talking with my friends because they've probably experienced or are experiencing the same problems. Even though my parents tell me I can talk to them about anything, there are some things I just don't think they would understand.'

Nicole, aged 15

Feelings

During puberty, our emotions can take us on a real rollercoaster ride. The 'ups' are happier than anything we have ever experienced before, but feelings such as sadness, loneliness or shyness are also far more intense. This affects all of our relationships, including those with our friends and people we would like to go out with.

When we just wish the floor would swallow us up, it's worth remembering that everyone has moments of extreme embarrassment.

It's your opinion

The way relationships between teens are featured in magazines and soaps can make us feel as though 'everybody's doing it'. Do you think these media may force some teenagers into roles they are not ready for? To what extent do you think our hormones play a part?

It's a chemical thing

It can be hard to handle highly-charged emotions, but they are perfectly normal. They are partly due to our pituitary gland, which produces our sex hormones. When this gland becomes active in puberty, the increased hormone levels affect our moods. It feels weird not being in control, but it does not last forever. As our bodies get used to all the hormones, our emotions settle down too.

Crushes

While our feelings race out of control, some of us develop a crush. It may seem a lot like the 'serious' or 'passionate' love we see between adults in books or films – we can't stop thinking about the person and may blush or stammer when we see him or her. But often the person is someone who could never return our feelings, for example, a pop star.

A crush can feel just like true love. Our heart leaps when we see the person and we just can't stop thinking about him or her.

Crushes can be embarrassing but perhaps, without us knowing it, they are important 'practice sessions'. They let us explore one-way passion before we have to cope with a two-way loving relationship.

Just good friends?

Relationships with close friends can be just as unsettling. It is confusing when someone we have been friends with for years is suddenly sexually attractive to us.

It can be easy to mistake strong attachment for sexual feelings but even if the attraction is real, we still have a choice whether to act on it. We might be too shy or not want to risk losing a friend. If we decide to come clean, we have to be prepared for rejection – or for the risks of taking the relationship to a whole new level.

It's your experience

'My [male] friend Ikenna and I have known each other for four years. Since we're close friends, people automatically assume something is up when we're together. They say that we can't be 'just friends' and eventually something sexual will happen between us.'

Melissa, aged 17

What sex is for

In many cultures and religions, the purpose of sex is to procreate, or produce children. This usually goes hand-in-hand with the belief that sex should happen only between a husband and wife. Other people believe that there is nothing wrong with people who are not married having sex. They may have sex to express their love and commitment, or just because it feels good.

With all the emotional factors to consider, it's easy to forget sex has a biological function – to produce new life.

Procreation

Often, our first knowledge of sex is as a means of making babies. We may even have once thought that our parents only ever had sex a few times, in order to make us – and our brothers or sisters.

As we get older, we learn that many people have sex without wanting to get pregnant. They may be couples who are happy with the number of children they already have, or people who do not want to be a parent yet – or ever.

It's your experience

▶ 'I wanted to wait but my boyfriend made me think it wasn't a big deal, so I did it. Immediately I regretted it. I was so upset and confused'.

Jane, aged 16

Sex without intercourse

Sex for procreation is simply about delivering the man's sperm to the woman's egg. It includes very little activity beyond intercourse - placing a penis inside a vagina. But many of us have a wider idea of what sex is about, from kissing and rubbing to a whole range of physical contacts. This sex is clearly not just about making babies.

When we fall in love, our emotions go haywire. It can be a challenge choosing not to have sex, but many couples enjoy just being close.

It's your experience

'We used protection and the timing felt right. Although we're not together anymore, we're still friendly and I'm glad that we shared our first times with one another.'

John, aged 17

Bringing people together

Kissing and petting are sexually arousing – they make us desire each other. This can be enjoyable in itself, or it can lead to intercourse. Many teenagers enjoy kissing and hugging their boyfriend or girlfriend and don't feel a need to go any further, perhaps for a long time.

Sex can satisfy our desires and, at the same time, help us to feel closer to each other, but only if we are emotionally ready for it. If not, having a sexual relationship can actually make us feel more isolated.

Other myths exploded

If we do decide to have sex, we should make sure it is for the right reasons. Sex won't make a man and woman of us, clear up a spotty face or make us more popular. Above all, it won't mend a relationship that is already going wrong.

One thing is certain, sex adds a new dimension to any relationship, and this has its pros and cons. The important thing is to stay true to our own feelings – but that's easier said than done.

Is sex just for procreation? Couples continue to enjoy sexual relationships, and the intimacy they bring, long after child-bearing age.

It's your opinion

Do you agree or disagree with the following ideas about sex:
• Sex without the chance of procreation is wrong, so I would never have sex before marriage.
• I would leave my boyfriend/girlfriend if I really wanted sex but they didn't.
• It is okay to have sex without love, so long as you are both open and honest.
• Even if you have got someone really excited, it's your right to stop.

Sexual orientation

For the majority of people, a sexual relationship means one between a man and a woman. Heterosexuality is the norm and our social structures favour and encourage this. However, this does not account for everyone. A small number of us find that we are attracted to people of our own sex, some people find both men and women sexually attractive – and some choose not to be sexual at all.

Same-sex relationships bring their own unique problems, including prejudice from some sections of society.

Being gay

Homosexuality comes from the Greek word *homo*, which means 'the same'. Some people prefer the words 'lesbian' (for women only) or 'gay' instead. First sexual feelings are confusing anyway, but even more so if we are attracted to people of our own sex.

In most of the Western world, homosexuality is no longer illegal (see page 36), but this does not mean that everyone accepts gay relationships and some people have religious beliefs that it is not acceptable.

It's your experience

'Now, everything is fine; my friends and family accept my sexuality and I'm living an open lifestyle. I never feel uncomfortable when people ask me if I'm gay, and I don't feel different anymore. Being gay is just a part of who I am; it's not me as a whole.'

Alexander, aged 17

In almost every country, heterosexuality is seen as the norm and marriage is permitted only between a man and a woman. Here, thousands of Moonies (followers of Sung Myung Moon) take part in a mass wedding.

It's your opinion

Scientists have observed homosexual behaviour between apes. How does this affect the argument that gay sexuality is not natural because it cannot produce children? If it is okay for heterosexuals to have sex to express love or for pleasure, is the same true for gays?

Bisexuality

Those of us who find both sexes attractive are called bisexuals. Since bisexuals experience different-sex and same-sex relationships, some people accuse them of being 'sex-mad'. However, bisexuals are no more or less sexually active than heterosexuals or homosexuals.

Those of us who are 'bi' are attracted to a person because of who they are as an individual, rather than because of what gender they happen to be.

Fixing on a sexual identity

Sexual identity is usually just something we accept, but some of us struggle to explain and come to terms with the way we are.

Some of us think our sexuality is determined by our genes, or that upbringing, and relationships with our parents, causes our sexual orientation.

Finally, some of us think that our sexual identity is up to us. According to this way of thinking, our sexuality is just what suits our personality, not something forced on us.

Deciding about sex

Once we start to have sexual feelings, it is up to us whether to act on them. We have to try to take the decision for ourselves. Pressures against us having sex may come from our parents or religious teachings. On the other hand, if we decide we do want to have sex, we need to be sure that it is not just because of pressures from our partner, peers, or even society as a whole.

Choosing virginity

A virgin is a person who has not had sex. In some places, youth groups are encouraging virginity and celibacy (not having sex). Some of us feel that sex can be devalued if it is not saved for our life-partner later on.

▼ When we are younger we may feel we are missing out on things. But as we grow up, feeling 'left out' is no reason to have sex if we don't feel ready.

By not having sex, we steer clear of unwanted pregnancy and sexually-transmitted infections (STIs), as well as the emotional demands of an intimate relationship. Banding together and pledging a commitment to virginity can also be a way to beat peer pressure.

Peer pressure

If everyone is talking about their sexual adventures, we can start to feel left out. However, research has shown that a lot more teens claim to have sexual experience than actually do. Even so, 'peer pressure' - the demands made on us by our friends - can be a positive thing, encouraging us to meet new challenges.

Pressure from a partner to have sex can be very wearing.

Yes or no?

Sex should only happen between two people who consent, or give their agreement. They should both be over the legal age as well (see page 35). Consent does not count if it is reluctantly given, or if it is given when someone is not in control of their behaviour, for example after drinking or taking illegal drugs.

Sex is nothing to be embarrassed about. If we feel unable to agree to sex unless we are 'loosened up' by drink, maybe we do not really want to have sex at all.

Partner pressure

Partners can pressurise us, too, for example by saying that if we really cared, we would have sex – or even that they might leave us if we won't. This can sometimes really wear us down.

It's your decision

If you don't want to have sex, be honest – and stick to your guns. It might help to practise some different ways of saying 'No' to sex, until you feel confident that you can clearly express how you feel. Here are some ideas – try to come up with some more:

'No. If you cared about me you wouldn't put pressure on me.'

'No. I don't feel we know each other well enough yet. I'll let you know when I'm ready.'

'No. It goes against my principles and I have to stay true to myself.'

'No. We need to talk about contraception first.'

Sam's birthday

We should be on guard after drinking. That's when we're most likely to be pushed into sex we don't want.

19

Sex in theory

At some time in our teens, or even before, our bodies start to change. In both girls and boys, our bodies become hairier and start to sweat more. We are changing from children into adult men and women. The developments in our bodies will, in most cases, make us able to have children. They will make us capable of sexual intercourse.

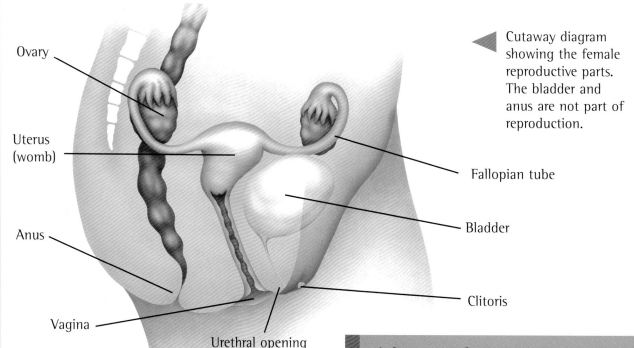

Ovary

Uterus (womb)

Anus

Vagina

Urethral opening

Fallopian tube

Bladder

Clitoris

Cutaway diagram showing the female reproductive parts. The bladder and anus are not part of reproduction.

From girl to woman

In girls, puberty means that our breasts swell and our ovaries start to release ova (eggs). At least one ovum ripens each month, and the lining of the uterus (womb) thickens in readiness to receive it if it is fertilised.

Usually, fertilisation and conception do not happen, so the ovum and uterus lining are shed. This is called menstruation, or having a period. It happens once a month and lasts between three and seven days.

It's your decision

Are you ready yet?
The changes in our bodies during puberty prepare us for having sex – and babies. Few teenagers are ready to cope with the responsibility of being a parent, but what about the responsibilities of a sexual relationship? Even if your body is 'ready', don't worry if you don't feel ready in your head yet.

Cutaway diagram showing the male reproductive parts. The bladder and anus are not part of reproduction.

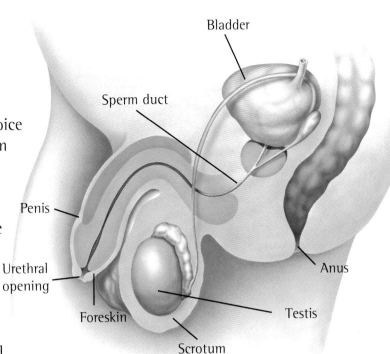

Bladder
Sperm duct
Penis
Urethral opening
Foreskin
Scrotum
Anus
Testis

From boy to man

In boys, puberty means that our voice deepens and our penis and scrotum become bigger. The scrotum is the loose pouch of skin that hangs below the penis. Inside it, our testicles, or testes, start to produce sperm. We have erections more often and are able to ejaculate.

Sexual intercourse

All of these changes are a preparation for having adult sexual relationships. During intercourse, the man's penis becomes hard and erect. The man then fits his penis into the woman's vagina.

When the man reaches orgasm, he ejaculates – a whitish liquid called semen is released from his penis. It contains millions of tiny sex cells, called sperm. If the couple are not using a barrier method of contraception (see page 26) some of the sperm 'swim' up through the uterus and into the Fallopian tubes. Here, they may meet an ovum.

Fertilisation

Fertilisation happens when a sperm and ovum join together. This does not happen every time a couple have unprotected sex but is always possible.

From the moment it is fertilised, the ovum keeps on dividing, in order to make more and more cells. The fertilised ovum travels down the Fallopian tube into the uterus. Here, it implants into the lining. This is called conception. Now the woman is pregnant.

It's your experience

'I don't always want sex. But because I'm a guy with a penis that often stiffens up, my girlfriend thinks that I want sex all the time. I just like to be close to her sometimes – that's all.'

David, aged 17

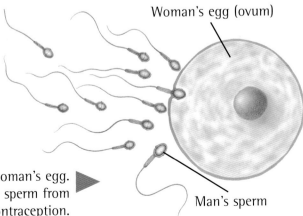

Woman's egg (ovum)

Man's sperm

The strongest sperm wins the race to fertilise the woman's egg. Immediately a barrier froms around the egg to stop other sperm from entering. Fertilisation can usually be avoided by using contraception.

Sex in practice

Knowing how sex works in theory is one thing, but knowing what it is like in practice is something else. That is because sex is all about sensation and emotion – and those are experiences that differ from person to person.

Kissing feels nice and brings intimacy. As kissing becomes more urgent, it can also arouse us and make us ready for sex.

Getting ready for sex

Before intercourse happens, a man and a woman need to become excited. They arouse each other with their mouths and hands, kissing and caressing. This is called foreplay. The man's penis becomes erect or stiff. The woman's vagina becomes slippery and more open and her clitoris swells.

For some couples, perhaps at the beginning of their relationship, this is enough for them and they don't feel the need to go further. You can learn a lot about yourself and your partner at this stage.

It's your opinion

Not every sexual experience leads to intercourse. Some people are happy to give each other sexual pleasure while staying 'virgins' as far as intercourse is concerned. Do you believe virginity is about not having intercourse, or about avoiding sexual contact in general?

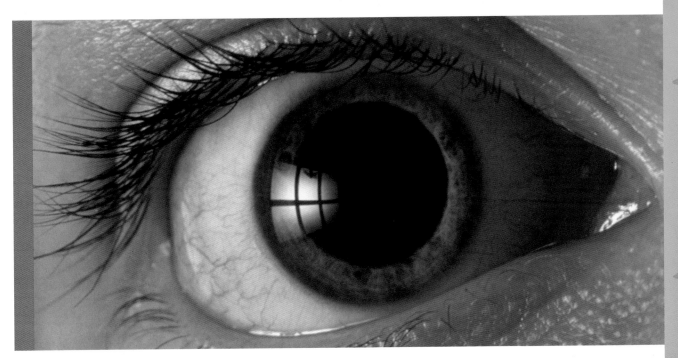

Sex in action

When they are both ready, the man slides his penis into the woman's vagina. He starts to move it back and forwards and the woman moves her hips. The rhythm can be fast, slow or a mix of the two – whatever feels most enjoyable.

The man and woman start to feel more and more pleasure and, eventually, they may have an orgasm. This is also called coming or climaxing.

Sexual climax

An orgasm is hard to describe. It is a sensation of intense pleasure that leaves the person feeling very happy, relaxed and satisfied. The man and woman do not necessarily have their orgasm at the same time – or at all.

When a man orgasms, he ejaculates. When a woman orgasms, her vagina may become extra-slippery. Many women are unable to reach orgasm through vaginal stimulation. They may need clitoral stimulation – rubbing of the clitoris.

▲ Arousal affects other parts of the body, not just the genitals. The excitement makes our pupils dilate, or grow bigger.

Sex by the book

There is no right or wrong way to have sex. Vaginal penetration need not happen at all and often does not – for example between same-sex couples, when one partner is disabled in some way, or simply because neither partner feels like it.

Between couples who do want penetrative sex, there are many different positions. Some stick to one that gives them particular pleasure, while others prefer to experiment.

It's your experience

'I'm scared about doing it wrong because I think, "What if she doesn't like it, but won't tell me, and then goes off and says how bad I was?" You just feel stupid.'

Bryce, aged 15

Pregnancy

It seems incredible to think that a single tiny male sex cell, a sperm, and female sex cell, an ovum, can divide and multiply to form a complex human baby made up of billions of cells. Pregnancy is amazing, but it is also something that should be planned for. It is important to be armed with all the facts.

Those of us who have sex but do not want a baby yet should always use birth control (see pages 26–27).

Conception

Conception is when a fertilised ovum (an egg joined with a sperm) implants itself into the thick wall of the uterus. This usually happens about three days after fertilisation – the time it takes for the ovum to travel down the fallopian tubes.

About five days after fertilisation, the embryo is a cluster of cells called a blastocyst. Soon it will embed itself in the wall of the uterus.

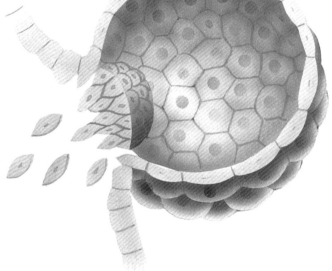

Signs of pregnancy

One of the first signs of pregnancy is a missed period. This is because the ovum has been fertilised, so the body does not shed it, or the uterus lining. Another early sign is morning sickness - feeling queasy, often in the morning, but sometimes at other times of the day.

It's possible to test for pregnancy from when the next period is due. Test sticks check urine for the hormone HCG, released by the embryo.

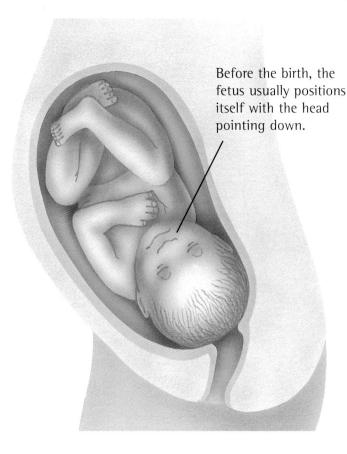

Before the birth, the fetus usually positions itself with the head pointing down.

After 40 weeks in the womb, the fetus is fully formed and ready to be born.

The developing baby

During the first eight weeks, the baby is called an embryo. It develops very fast. By six weeks, its brain and spine are forming. After eight weeks, the baby is known as a fetus. By 12 weeks it looks human, with arms, legs and facial features. A protective sac filled with fluid has formed around the fetus. At around 40 weeks, the mother goes into labour. This is a period of around 12 to 15 hours during which the baby is born.

Abortion

In many parts of the world, it is possible to end an unwanted pregnancy by having an abortion. This is when a doctor causes a deliberate miscarriage.

If the baby is developing abnormally or the mother's health is threatened, abortion may be possible at any stage in the pregnancy. Otherwise, it is usually illegal to abort after a certain stage of development – for example, 24 weeks in the UK. In a few countries and some US states, abortion is illegal at any stage of a pregnancy.

Contraction

For those of us who want to have sex without becoming pregnant, there are many birth control options. The most common are the pill and condoms. Contraception is a responsibility for both partners, so which method to use is a decision to share.

There are condoms designed for both male and female use. For now, the pill can only be taken by women, but the male pill is in development.

Diaphragm

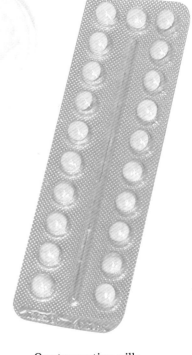

Barrier methods

The simplest means of contraception is a barrier between the sperm and ova. The condom, unrolled on to the erect penis, is most popular. Every packet of condoms comes with advice on how to use a condom properly, which should be read carefully. Used properly, condoms are extremely effective. As well as preventing pregnancy they also protect against STIs (see pages 28–29). However, they can sometimes split, releasing sperm and making pregnancy or infection possible.

Condom

Contraceptive pills

Barrier methods for women include the female condom, the diaphragm or 'cap' and the contraceptive sponge. The cap is a re-usable barrier available from the doctor. It is placed in the vagina before sex and must be used with spermicidal (sperm-killing) creams, foams or pessaries.

It's your decision

Which contraception method is appropriate for you?
To make an informed decision, talk to your doctor or visit a family planning clinic. Here you will be able to get free condoms and spermicides as well as prescription contraceptives, such as the pill or the cap.

Contraceptive pills

Used properly, the pill is the most effective contraceptive, but it poses a risk to some women and some others experience side effects. In addition, it does not offer protection against disease as condoms do.

Birth control pills are prescribed by a doctor. There are two main types. The combined pill is taken once a day for three weeks of every month. It contains low doses of oestrogen and progestogen that prevent ovulation (the monthly release of eggs). The mini-pill or progestogen-only pill has less impact on the body, which is good for women with other health risks. It alters the wall of the cervix so sperm cannot enter.

Researchers are working on a male pill and on pills for women which are taken without a break between packs.

Other methods

Devices such as the coil (called an Intra-Uterine Device, or IUD) are fitted into the uterus and can stay in for several years.

Other possibilities are injections and implants that release progestogen into the body. None of these methods is recommended for young women.

Emergency contraception

Sometimes a couple forget to use contraception or their usual method goes wrong – for example, a condom splits.

Depending on the laws where they live, the woman may be able to take an Emergency Contraceptive Pill (ECP) up to 72 hours after intercourse, but it should not be relied on as a regular contraceptive. As well as causing nausea and dizziness, it disrupts the user's bleeding pattern (and may pose other health risks).

The contraceptive pill should be taken at the same time each day. Missing a pill can increase the risk of getting pregnant. It is important to read very carefully the instructions that come with contraceptive pills.

It's your experience

'The people there were really nice to me. They gave me a pregnancy test and had me sign some forms. They assured me that they would not contact my parents.'

Nicole, aged 17
(on visiting a clinic for the morning-after pill in a US State which permits this practice)

Disease prevention

Pregnancy is not the biggest risk that we face when we have sex. Most importantly, we have to take steps to protect ourselves against sexually-transmitted infections (STIs) – infections passed on during sex. The only sure way to avoid them is to not have sex. However, we can minimise the risk of infection by using condoms. This is important even if we are certain that our partner is infection-free.

These are the daily drugs taken by a person with HIV/AIDS. They only reduce the symptoms. There is no cure for the disease.

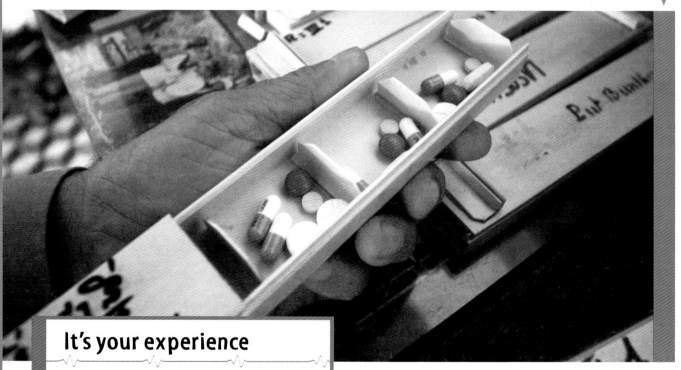

It's your experience

'I was diagnosed with genital herpes last year. I remember sitting next to the phone, praying my test results would come back negative. I had always thought herpes was some nasty disease only prostitutes could get.'

Anon (NO NAME OR AGE GIVEN)

Viruses

STIs caused by viruses include HIV/AIDS (Human Immunodeficiency Virus/Acquired Immunodeficiency Disease), genital warts or HPV (Human Papillomavirus), herpes and hepatitis B. HIV/AIDS affects the body's disease-fighting immune system and can be fatal. HIV can be passed on through heterosexual sex as well as homosexual sex.

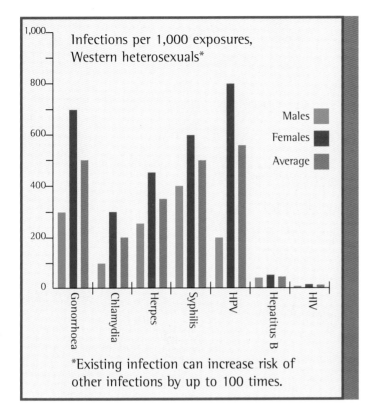

Infections per 1,000 exposures, Western heterosexuals*

Males
Females
Average

Gonorrhoea | Chlamydia | Herpes | Syphilis | HPV | Hepatitus B | HIV

*Existing infection can increase risk of other infections by up to 100 times.

Warts can be treated and hepatitis B can be prevented with a vaccine. There is no known cure yet for HIV/AIDS, herpes or hepatitis B. However, scientists are working on treatments and have already come up with drugs that can reduce the symptoms of these diseases.

Other types of STIs

Gonorrhoea, syphilis and chlamydia are bacterial infections that can be treated with antibiotics. However, people with chlamydia often show no symptoms. If the disease goes untreated it can lead to infertility.

Pubic lice, or 'crabs', are insect parasites that can be treated with insecticides. Candidiasis, or 'thrush', is a yeast infection. It is treatable with a fungicide.

It's your experience

'When the tests were being performed, I definitely felt awkward and a little embarrassed. But everyone made everything seem normal. Hey, maybe it was. It's just not something I'm used to. I realise, too, how important it is be responsible and healthy.'
Brad (no age given)
(after visiting an STI clinic for tests)

Getting help

STI symptoms can include pain when passing urine or having sex, unusual discharge from the vagina or penis, itchiness, skin rashes or sore lumps around the genitals.

However, not all STIs have symptoms, so it can be a good idea for us to visit a doctor or STI clinic if we have had unprotected sex. The medical staff will often give confidential tests and advice. Of course, it is much better not to let things get to that stage, by always wearing a condom when we have sex, even if the woman is on the pill.

Most clinics offer counselling if you test positive for an STI. They also give advice on how to break the news to past sexual partners.

Sex in relationships

Sex is rarely a one-off experience. For most of us, it is one of the most important ways that we express love in our relationship. Sex brings greater intimacy. In this close environment, we soon get over any initial worries, fears or embarrassments. Now we can face the joys and problems that an ongoing sexual relationship brings.

Sex brings intimacy, but cuddling and holding hands can also help us to feel close – and so can sharing our feelings.

It's your opinion

Sex is not the only aspect of a relationship that brings us together. Good communication and shared interests are important, too. Couples that choose not to have sex may find they pay more attention to other areas of their relationship and end up being closer than sexually-active couples. How important do you think sex is for achieving a loving partnership?

Taking time

For some of us, our first sexual experiences may be disappointing. Girls, in particular, may not feel the sexual 'fireworks' they were expecting, although they may still enjoy the feeling of closeness that sex brings. Boys may feel unable to prolong the sexual experience.

As we become more relaxed with our partner, and gain experience, there is less pressure. We can take our time to discover what things we like best.

Relationship rules

When we consent to sex, we are only agreeing to sex on that occasion. If we decide that we want time out – or to stop altogether – that is perfectly all right. The process of learning through experience continues as adults, but our teenage years are when new experiences shape our character most of all. This affects all our relationships, not just our sexual ones.

Talking it over

Sex is a private thing between two individuals. However, it is good if we can be honest with our parents - they are usually the most helpful adults we have to support us. Being open can also help to build up trust. Most parents worry when they suspect their children have started to have sex. They do not need any of the private details, but it can reassure them to know that we are facing our responsibilities and taking care to avoid the risks of disease or pregnancy. They will see that we are acting like responsible adults.

It's your experience

'My boyfriend and I went out for ten months and both of us were completely honest with each other. We took time in the beginning of our relationship to get to know each other before trying anything physical, which helped us connect emotionally.'

Crystal, aged 17

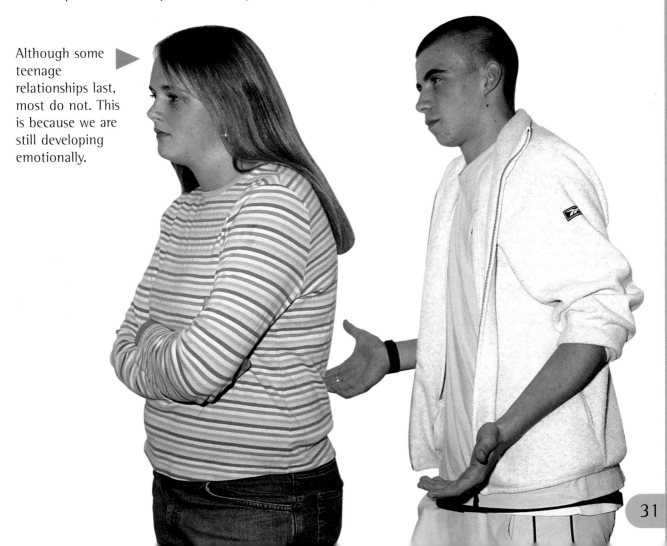

Although some teenage relationships last, most do not. This is because we are still developing emotionally.

Young parents

Teenagers who become pregnant have limited options open to them, but there are still choices. If abortion is not available, or against our beliefs, then we will have to carry through with the pregnancy, whether we want the baby or not. After giving birth, some teens give up their babies to adoptive parents, feeling that this will give them the best chance in life. Others decide to keep the child.

Single parents

Although a pregnancy is caused by two people, the baby grows inside the mother's body. Boys can walk away from the responsibility but girls cannot. Often, a pregnant girl may have to bring up her child alone. More rarely, the father may choose to bring up the child. Being a single parent is hard enough for adults. As teenagers, we lack emotional maturity and financial independence. Single parents need lots of support from family and friends.

Working it out together

Some couples face parenthood together. Depending on our own feelings – and the views of our parents – we may get married or move in together. If we are still at school, we have to consider how we will support ourselves, especially if our parents cannot help out.

Parenthood will bring strains, such as money worries, lack of sleep or blaming each other. Our relationship may not survive. Any future relationship we have will be affected by being a parent.

It's your experience

'I get pictures and letters every six months. So I'm involved, even though I'm not struggling to raise him. I wanted both my son and me to have lives that we deserve and not be deprived.'

Jen, aged 17, who got pregnant aged 14 and put her son up for adoption

A teenage relationship can survive the strain of parenthood, but it takes a lot of hard work. In most cases, the parents split up.

It's your decision

How do you think our ideas about parenthood match up with the reality? It's good to think through what we would do – but none of us can be certain how we will react until the situation arises. How do your decisions compare to the ones made by the US teenagers in the chart opposite?

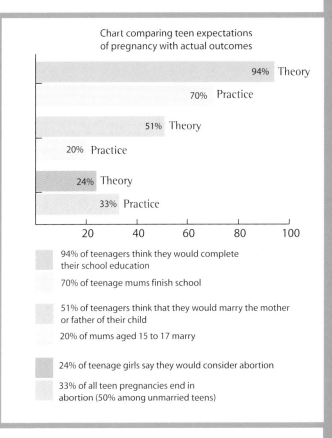

Chart comparing teen expectations of pregnancy with actual outcomes

94%	Theory
70%	Practice
51%	Theory
20%	Practice
24%	Theory
33%	Practice

94% of teenagers think they would complete their school education

70% of teenage mums finish school

51% of teenagers think that they would marry the mother or father of their child

20% of mums aged 15 to 17 marry

24% of teenage girls say they would consider abortion

33% of all teen pregnancies end in abortion (50% among unmarried teens)

A life-changing experience

As teenage parents, we give up freedoms such as buying what we want or going out with friends. We may miss out on further education. There is also the responsibility of caring for the child.

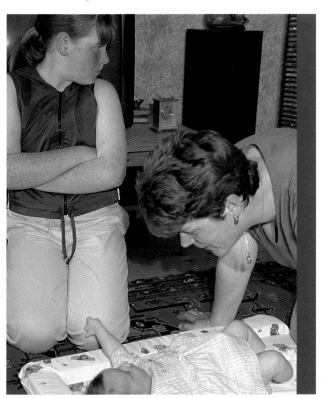

Family support brings its own problems. A young mum who is still going to school may feel left out by her own mum's relationship with the baby.

However, there are some good sides, too. Our parents are likely to be active and supportive grandparents, for example. We will still be relatively young when our children 'leave the nest'. And we can avoid the fertility problems sometimes faced by people who have waited before starting a family.

It's your experience

'My mum wanted to help me take care of him a lot. But I felt she wasn't helping me, but taking away from me being his father. With this came difficulties. How could she help without taking over? She wanted to protect me, but also give me room to raise him.'

Scott, aged 17
(who was 14 when his son Josh was born)

Law and age

One of the most annoying things about being a teenager can be the way that we are treated as children by the law, even when we know we are more like adults than 'real' kids.

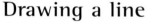

It doesn't matter how grown-up we feel. In the eyes of the law, teenagers below a certain age are children.

Drawing a line

The law has to draw a line between adults and children. It is useful for making sure that we receive the support and protection we need as children. The line is also there to protect adult freedoms – it makes clear that from a certain age onwards, each of us is responsible for our own life, and that no one has the right to interfere with our legal choices.

Locating the line

In most countries, the age we legally become adults is set at around 16 years old. Usually, there are laws for particular things, such as alcohol use, or voting, which limit our freedom as adults until we are 18 or 21 years old.

We all see that some people grow up more quickly than others, but the law is not allowed to judge people like this, unless a learning disability causes them a measurable delay in development.

It's your opinion

Different countries have different rules about when we should be allowed the freedom to make our own choices. For example, look at the different treatment of gay people. Do you think it is good for different societies to have different rules about young people, or does this seem unfair? Should children have rights that every culture is forced to follow?

It's your experience

'I'm not sure what I was thinking. I guess I felt lucky that Gabe actually liked me. I didn't ask him to stop because I was afraid he'd stop liking me and leave.'

Jennifer, aged 17 (who had sex with a 21-year-old when she was 12)

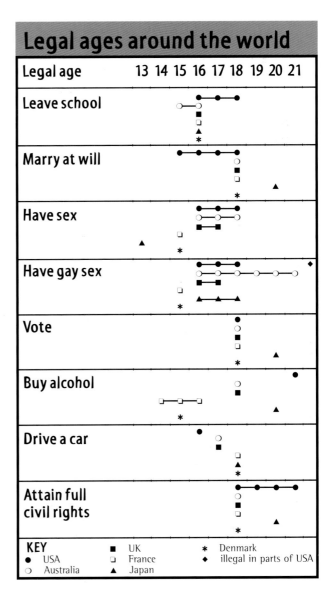

Counsellors listen to our problems and give unbiased advice. Anything we say to a counsellor is usually kept confidential.

It's your experience

'I never thought about the risks or consequences. Having sex just sort of happened.'

Brittany, aged 14

Useful rules

The rules about when we are allowed to have sex may vary a little from country to country, but they are there for the same general reasons. They remind children that they may lack the experience to think through the issues and risks involved. They remind parents to take care of their children's welfare.

They also prevent confused adults from abusing children sexually. Adults who use minors for sex are committing a serious crime. The law is strict about this, to protect children from harm.

Sex before the legal age

Laws against underage sex are mainly to prevent confused adults from harming children – these laws are less likely to be applied to two minors of the same age.

You will not get into trouble with the law if you want to talk to an adult about a sex-related problem before you are at the legal age.

Legal ages around the world

Legal age	13	14	15	16	17	18	19	20	21
Leave school			○	●■□▲*	●	●			
Marry at will				●	●	●○■*	□		▲
Have sex		▲	□*	●○■	●○■	○			
Have gay sex			□*	●○▲	●■▲	●○▲	○	○	○ ◆
Vote						●○■□*		▲	
Buy alcohol				□ □ □ *		○■		▲	●
Drive a car			●	○■□▲*					
Attain full civil rights				●○■□*	●	●	●	▲	

KEY

- ● USA
- ○ Australia
- ■ UK
- □ France
- ▲ Japan
- * Denmark
- ◆ illegal in parts of USA

Law and sex

The laws of different places express the values of each society – our beliefs about right and wrong. The values a society has about sex are among the most powerful there are – they affect how we raise and educate children, how we organise families, and even how we deal with quite distant issues, such as how property is divided up. In most societies we now have rights, which allow us the freedom and privacy to be how we choose to be, even when that differs from what the majority may want.

Sex itself

Different types of sex and sexual relationship are banned under some laws, independently of the specific age of the people involved. For example, some countries have laws banning those employed to educate older teens from forming any sexual relationship with students.

Many countries have laws which allow certain forms of sexual relationship at a younger age than others – female/female relationships are often not banned at all, while male/male relationships may be more limited than male/female ones.

Sharia law is a code of living followed by some Muslims. Offences under the law include any sex outside marriage. Few countries enforce this law, however.

Parents are legally responsible for their children, but not all parents find it easy to talk to their children to ensure they are safe.

Non-consensual sex

Even if both parties are old enough to consent to sex, there are still situations where sex is against the law. Rape is when someone has sexual intercourse with another person who has not consented, or agreed, to sex. Rape is illegal.

We usually think of rapists as violent strangers, but most rapes are committed by people who know their victim. Any sexual act that one party does not want is a rape.

It's your experience

'It's not normal, whether it's two guys or two girls. I'm a strong believer in the Bible and in my religion and they say not to accept gays. I think it is wrong, because that is what God teaches'.

Kyle, no age given

Parenting

Parents are legally responsible for their children - to look after them and help them reach adulthood in good physical and mental health. In some cases, parents can be punished when children are not supported properly. In the UK, for example, parents can now be sent to prison if they repeatedly fail to get their child to attend school.

Parents and the law

Parents usually have a legal right to forbid certain types of sex education for their child at school. In the UK parents can withdraw their children from some lessons.

It's your experience

'I don't think anyone can decide what is normal'.

Jessica, no age given

Talking to friends

During our teens, many of us retain our best friends but also start hanging out in larger groups. We choose our friends, and tend to go for people who share the same interests, hopes and opinions. We do lots of activities together, so we are exposed to similar experiences. For these reasons it is usually a good idea to share our problems and give each other advice. That is what being a good friend is all about.

A sleepover is a good opportunity to swap advice and share feelings with a friend.

Respect!

We should always be sensitive about our friends' experiences and problems. They may not enjoy living through our every problem in minute detail. They may even feel uncomfortable if we are too open.

We should also remember that sex is an intimate experience. Before talking about it – even with our best friends – we should consider how we would feel if it was our partner talking about us.

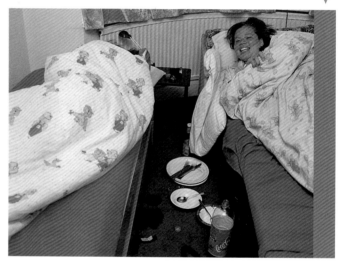

Myths to watch out for

During teenagehood, we are all learning. That includes our friends, however knowledgeable they appear. Just because someone sounds as if they know what they are talking about, it does not mean they really do.

Talking to friends can help, but remember their advice might not always be right!

It's your decision

What do you do if new relationships affect your friendships?

At some point, you may fall in love with the same person as your best friend. Is it a good idea to share your feelings? By talking things over, you can decide whether either of you will try to go out with that person, or whether it's just not worth it. Then again, what if your friend starts going out with that person? You might be happier if they do not know your secret feelings.

Some people, for example, say that it is impossible to get pregnant the first time we have sex – but that is not true. Conception can happen even if we don't have an orgasm, and even if we are 'careful' – that is, withdraw the penis from the vagina before ejaculation. Pregnancy can happen at any time in the menstrual cycle, even during a girl's period.

It's your opinion

How important is it to you to stand on your own two feet? Do you feel too independent to take advice from other people – and believe that the only way you'll learn is to make mistakes? Or are you happier avoiding the mistakes and benefiting from your friends' experiences – even if that make you less independent?

One of the silliest myths about sex is that you cannot get pregnant if you have sex standing up. Fertilisation can happen in any position.

Sharing emotions

Of course it is fine to share information with friends, but all of this is available in books or from experienced adults. Friends are best for when we want to talk about feelings. They see us socialising, so they have the clearest view of our relationships. They are likely to understand if we are confused, frightened or heartbroken. Friends of the opposite sex can help us to better understand where our partners are 'coming from'.

Talking to adults

Despite the generation gap, it really can be useful to talk to adults about sex and relationships. They were young once, and almost certainly faced the same problems that we face today. They also have a lot more experience than us. The other advantage of talking to adults, especially our parents, is that they are not very likely to gossip about us – whereas friends might.

One way to feel less awkward is to talk while sharing a task, like making dinner. It helps to have something to do with our hands.

Making the first move

Sex can be an awkward topic to talk about, so it makes sense to pick your moment carefully. It's easiest to talk about things generally, rather than to charge right in to talk about their experiences, or our own.

TV programmes or newspaper reports often raise issues to do with sex. We can use these as springboards to start a discussion and to find out our parents views about things.

It's your opinion

Some of us think adults should be allowed their privacy, while others believe adults shouldn't be embarrassed to talk about this stuff. It's best to let them choose their own level of privacy. Instead of asking, 'Have you ever had an unwanted pregnancy?', we can ask, 'What do you think about abortion?' That way, they can decide how much they share of their own experiences.

Parents and other adults

Most parents are reasonable human beings. They also have our best interests at heart. They will usually be pleased that we feel we can be open with them and happy to give us the benefit of their knowledge.

It's easier all-round to involve our parents in our lives, but some of us know that our parents will not be able to support us in difficult situations. Fortunately, there are clinics and doctors that can help whether or not our parents are involved (see contacts on page 43).

If we can't talk to our parents, there are other sources of reliable information. Advice centres and clinics produce useful leaflets, for example.

It's your experience

'Many people say it's important for your parents to sit down and have a sex talk with you, but I don't agree. Although my parents did not have a talk with me, they informed me in other ways – with books and little titbits of knowledge. My experiences with them really helped me to form my own, informed opinions, which are not just their opinions drummed into my brain'

Emily, aged 16

In many countries, such as the UK, doctors will give contraceptive advice and treatment to girls who are under the age of consent.

Pair of ears

If we cannot talk to our parents, there are other people we can turn to – an aunt or uncle, a teacher or school counsellor. They can offer us impartial advice and help us to find solutions to any problems we face.

In the end, however, it's our health and we are responsible for ourselves. We have to weigh up advice from adults, books and information leaflets and friends, and see how it fits in with our own feelings and beliefs.

Glossary

Abortion deliberately ending a pregancy by medical intervention

Arousing sexually exciting

Barrier method form of contraception that places a barrier between sperm and egg, for example a condom

Bisexuality being sexually attracted to both sexes

Celibacy not having sexual relationships

Commitment promises to each other

Conception when a fertilised ovum (egg) implants in the lining of the uterus (womb)

Contraception prevention of pregnancy

Devalued made less special

Ejaculate when a penis emits semen

Erection a penis that has enlarged and grown hard, because it is aroused

Fertilisation when a sperm and ovum (egg) join together to create the beginnings of a new life

Gene one of the tiny 'instructions' contained within a molecule of DNA that builds a human body

Genitals sexual organs

Heterosexuality being sexually attracted to the opposite sex

Homosexuality being sexually attracted to the same sex

Hormone chemicals produced by special glands in the body that carry messages to particular organs or tissues

Impartial not favouring one particular viewpoint; unbiased

Infertility inability to produce a child

Menstruation shedding of the lining of the uterus, roughly every 28 days if fertilisation has not occurred

Minor someone who has not reached the age of majority, that is, the age of being legally an adult. Minors are also sometimes described as 'under-age'

Oestrogen a female sex hormone that prepares the woman for ovulation (the release of an ovum from a Fallopian tube). Oestrogen is used in the combined contraceptive pill

Penetrative sex a sexual act where one partner's penis enters the other partner's body, for example through the vagina

Procreation producing children

Progestogen a type of female sex hormone that builds up the lining of the uterus, ready to receive a fertilised ovum. Progestogen is used in contraceptive pills

Puberty the period of a person's life when their body is sexually maturing

Sexually-transmitted infection (STI) any infection that is passed on through sexual contact, for example HIV/AIDS

Sexual orientation whether we are heterosexual, homosexual or bisexual

Underage sex sex where one or both partners is a minor

Unprotected sex sex without contraception to prevent pregnancy

Virginity the state of never having had sexual intercourse

Further information

UK
Brook Online
The Brook provides free, confidential sex advice and contraception to young people.
www.brook.org.uk

fpa
Works to improve sexual health and campaigns to improve birth control.
www.fpa.org.uk

Local Advice Centres
A website where you can key in your town and select an area of help, such as 'sexuality and sexual health'.
www.thesite.org/info/in_your_area/

Sex: Are you thinking about it enough?
A website for under-18s with facts and advice on all aspects of sex.
www.ruthinking.co.uk

Facts of life
Advice on sex, puberty and more from the UK's National Grid for Learning.
www.factsoflife.org.uk

Australia
NSW Health
Information on sexually-transmitted diseases and safe sex practices.
www.health.nsw.gov.au/health-public-affairs/publications/std/contents.html

Queensland Health Youth Site
A government site aimed at adolescents and focusing on safe sex and relationships.
www.istaysafe.com

fpa
Family planning links, information and emergency advice.
www.fpa.net.au/about.htm

Sex! Life! (Victoria)
Click on 'Youth Centre' for Family Planning.
www.sexlife.net.au

New Zealand
fpa
Information on sex, life and relationships advice and information.
www.theword.org.nz

Urge
Introductory advice from an independent website backed by the government.
www.urge.org.nz/sex/relationships.html

Other info:
Stand Up Girl
A site with encouraging experiences of teenage pregnancy and motherhood. It has an anti-abortion agenda.
www.standupgirl.com

Note to parents and teachers: Because of the nature of the subject matter and the Internet, these websites may contain material that is inappropriate for some children. We therefore strongly advise that Internet access is supervised by a responsible adult.

Index

44

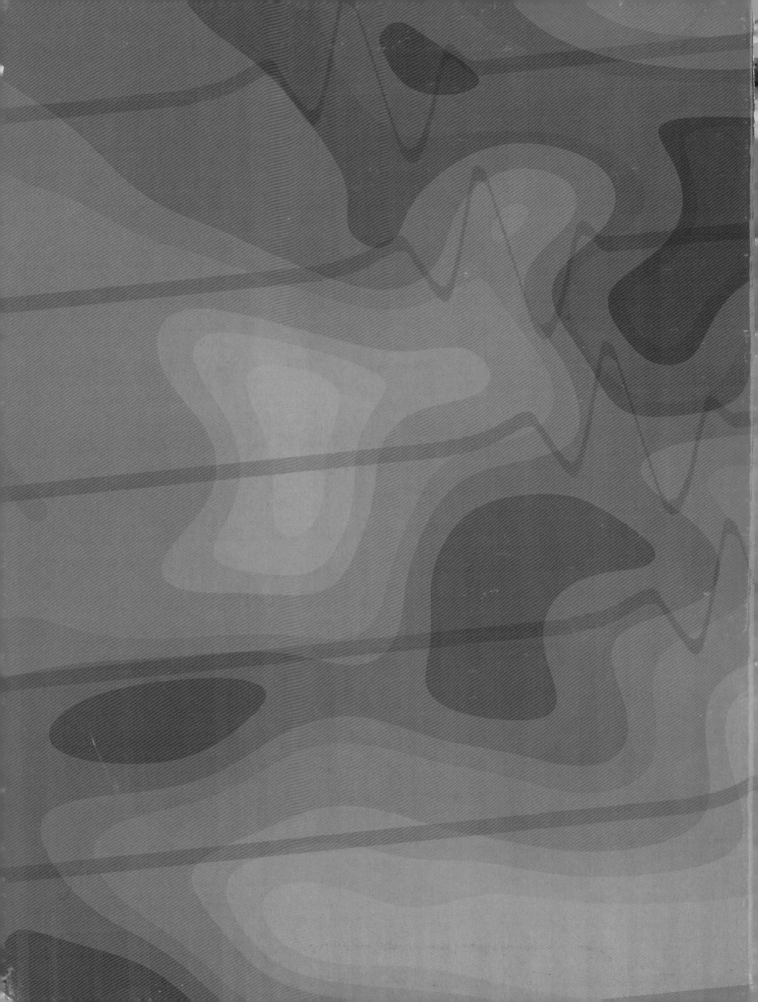